The Life and Work of...

Henry Moore

Sean Connolly

Heinemann
LIBRARY

First published in Great Britain by
Heinemann Library,
Halley Court, Jordan Hill, Oxford OX2 8EJ
a division of Reed Educational and Professional
Publishing Ltd.
Heinemann is a registered trademark of Reed
Educational & Professional Publishing Ltd.

OXFORD MELBOURNE AUCKLAND
JOHANNESBURG BLANTYRE GABORONE
IBADAN PORTSMOUTH (NH) USA CHICAGO

Designed by Celia Floyd
Originated by Dot Gradations
Printed in Hong Kong/China

03 02 01 00 99
10 9 8 7 6 5 4 3 2 1

ISBN 0 431 09179 X

British Library Cataloguing in Publication Data

Connolly, Sean
   Life and work of Henry Moore
   1. Moore, Henry, 1898-1986 – Juvenile literature
   2. Artists – England – Biography – Juvenile literature
   3. Art, Modern – 20th century – England – Juvenile
   literature
   I. Title
   730.9'2

For more information about Heinemann Library
books, or to order, please telephone
+44(0)1865 888066, or send a fax to +441865 314091.
You can visit our web site at www.heinemann.co.uk

Acknowledgements

The Publishers would like to thank the following for
permission to reproduce photographs:

The Henry Moore Foundation for:

Page 4, 'Portrait Studio, 1960'. Page 5, Henry
Moore 'Three Forms: Vertebrae'. Page 6, Henry
Moore aged 11. Page 7, Castleford Grammar
School's Roll of Honour. Page 8, Henry Moore
convalescing at Castleford Grammar School, 1918.
Page 9, Henry Moore 'Small Animal Head 1921'.
Page 10, Corner of Studio Adie Road 1928. Page 11,
Henry Moore 'Reclining Figure 1929'. Page 12,
Henry Moore with West Wind 1928. Page 13, North
wall of Headquarters of London Underground.
Page 14, Corner of studio at 11a Parkhill Road
Hampstead 1936. Page 15, Henry Moore 'Reclining
Figure 1936'. Page 17, Henry Moore 'Two forms
1934'. Page 18, Lee Miller, Henry Moore in Holborn
Underground, London 1943. Page 19, Henry Moore
'Pink and Green Sleepers 1941'. Page 20, Lee Miller
Archives, Henry Moore with Severini in Venice for
the Biennale 1948. Page 21, Henry Moore
'Madonna and child'. Page 22, Henry Moore
carving UNESCO Reclining Figure 1957-58. Page 23
Henry Moore 'Draped Reclining Figure 1952-53'.
Page 24, Henry Moore in Top Studio 1954. Page 25,
Henry Moore 'Double Oval'. Page 26, Henry Moore
working in new maquette studio 1978. Page 27,
Henry Moore 'Sheep Piece 1962-63'. Page 28, The
Independent. Page 29, Henry Moore 'Large Figure
in a shelter 1952-53'.

Page 16, Robert Harding Picture Library.

Cover photograph reproduced with permission of
Bridgeman Art library

Our thanks to Paul Flux for his comments in the
preparation of this book and to Emma Stower at
the Henry Moore Foundation for all her help with
the picture selection.

Every effort has been made to contact copyright
holders of any material reproduced in this book.
Any omissions will be rectified in subsequent
printings if notice is given to the Publisher.

Any words appearing in the text in bold, **like this**,
are explained in the Glossary.

Contents

Who was Henry Moore?

Henry Moore was one of the most important artists of this century. He made huge **sculptures** out of stone, wood and **bronze**. He also made many drawings.

People from around the world asked Henry to make sculptures for them. This sculpture, made in 1978, stands in Dallas, USA.

Early years

Henry Moore was born on 30 July 1898 in Castleford, England. His father was a **miner**. When Henry was 12 years old he won a **scholarship** to Castleford Grammar School.

Henry was already good at art. When he was 16 years old his teachers asked him to **carve** this **roll of honour** for the school.

London

Henry fought in the **First World War** for two years. In 1921 he began studying at the Royal College of Art in London. Two years later he visited Paris.

Henry saw many types of art in London and Paris. Henry made this **sculpture** of a small animal head in London in 1921.

Settling in

In 1925 Henry became a teacher at the Royal College of Art in London. He was also busy making his own **sculptures**. In 1928 he had a one-man **exhibition** in London.

Henry **carved** his sculptures out of stone. He liked to show people lying on their side. He made many more sculptures like this one.

The public eye

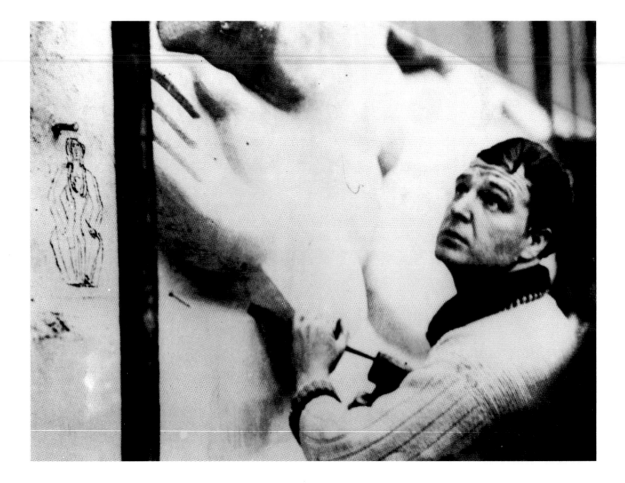

Henry became more famous. When he was 31 he did his first **commission**. It was a huge **sculpture** for the London Underground.

The title of this sculpture was *The North Wind*.
It shows Henry's interest in stone, fire, water
and wind.

The modern world

In the 1930s Henry became interested in **abstract art**. His **sculpture** began to look less like human beings and more like simple, rounded shapes.

Henry collected pebbles, stones and shells to see how Nature creates shapes. This statue shows Henry's interest in smooth, curved surfaces.

Getting known

More and more people saw the beauty in Henry's large **sculptures**. They were **exhibited** in Europe and the USA. This is a picture of the Museum of Modern Art in New York, USA.

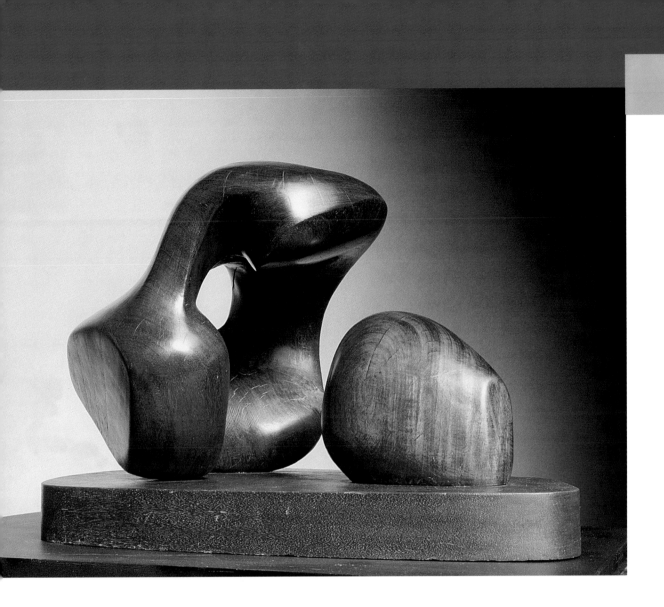

Henry sold this sculpture to the Museum of Modern Art in New York, USA. It shows how his sculptures were only partly **abstract**. Here you can still see human shapes.

War artist

The **Second World War** began in 1939. Two years later Henry was asked to become an official war artist. He drew the daily life of people in London during the war.

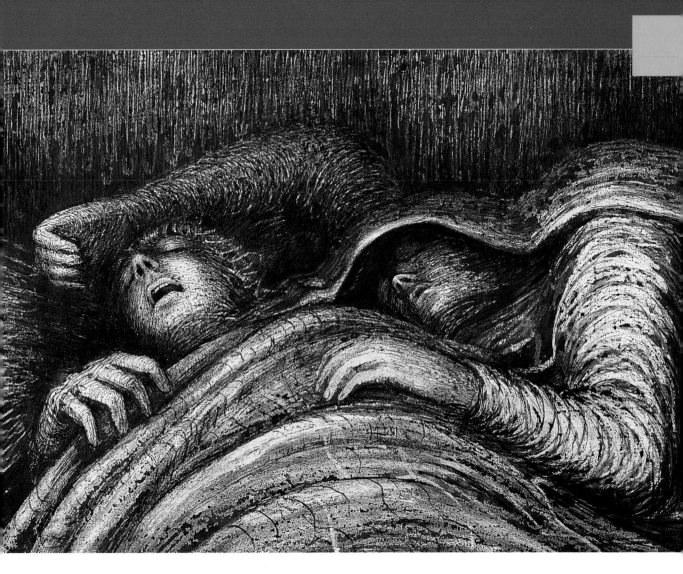

These drawings are some of Henry's most powerful works. This one shows people trying to sleep while bombs explode outside.

Travelling the world

After the war Henry travelled to many places. He got many awards and prizes for his **sculptures**. This picture shows Henry and a friend in Venice, Italy.

Henry's prizes did not change his way of thinking. He made this **tender** sculpture of Mary and Jesus for a church in Suffolk.

Time for a change

In the 1950s Henry tried new ways of working. Until then he **carved** directly from stone. Now he made many **sculptures** from **bronze** and wood.

22

Henry could make even bigger, smoother sculptures out of bronze. This sculpture of a woman is in front of a building in London.

New ideas

Henry also looked for new ideas. In the 1960s he began putting one shape inside another one. Many of these combined shapes created **hollow sculptures**.

Henry wanted people to look at his large sculptures from all sides. These two oval shapes seem alike at first. They only look different when you walk around them.

The sculptor's studio

Henry moved to Perry Green in Hertfordshire when London was bombed during the war. He was very happy there.

Sheep **grazed** in the field outside Henry's **studio**. In the 1970s Henry made many sketches of the sheep. He made this sculpture to go in the field.

An active life ends

Henry still worked when he was more than 80 years old. A special service in Westminster Abbey honoured Henry after his death on 31 August 1986.

Mourning Henry Moore yesterday: Jeremy Thorpe; Lord Snowdon and Sir Hugh Casson; Moore's daughter Mary Danowski and her children; Michael Foot and his wife, Jill Craigie.

Friends pay tribute to Moore

FELLOW ARTISTS and friends of the sculptor Henry Moore paid their last respects at a memorial service in Westminster Abbey yesterday. Many of his surviving contemporaries including his widow, Irina, whom he married in 1929, were too frail to attend.

Sir Stephen Spender, the poet, told the congregation that Moore, who died in August, aged 88, was the seventh son of a Yorkshire miner who never considered anyone either socially superior or inferior to himself.

Sir Stephen, one of the last surviving members of Moore's avant-garde Hamp-stead artistic circle in the Thirties, delivered the address in a brisk, husky whisper. He remembered Moore's studio as a focal point for artists, including Ben Nicholson, the painter, and Barbara Hepworth, the sculptress.

He said that despite Moore's admiration for the abstract artists around him, "he told me he could never make an artefact which referred to nothing but itself".

Moore had confided to him: "Try as I might, my work always ended up looking like something, probably a reclining figure."

Sir Stephen quoted Sir Herbert Read, the poet and art critic, and a champion of Moore in the Thirties, saying that in his opinion the sculptor would have been the best possible ambassador from this planet to another.

Sir Stephen said: "He was an artist of great ingenuity and a man of great humanity." Moore had never forgotten the simplicity of his upbringing.

Dame Peggy Ashcroft, the actress, read the first lesson, not from the Bible but from the Apocrypha, the second book of Esdras. It concluded: "He who made all things, and searcheth out hidden things in hidden places, surely he knoweth your imagination, and what ye think in your hearts." The text was suggested to the Moore family by Westminster Abbey, because its words were so appropriate.

The second lesson, read by the Duke of Gloucester, was from Revelations, in the King James version, chosen because it is the one familiar to Moore's generation.

The congregation included the Prime Minister; Michael Foot, the former Labour leader; Sir Hugh Casson, the architect and painter; Sir Roy Strong, director of the Victoria and Albert Museum; Jeremy Thorpe, the former Liberal leader; John Profumo, the former Conservative Cabinet minister, Lord Snowdon and Sam Wanamaker, the film maker.

List of mourners, page 13

28

This **sculpture** is the largest **bronze** work that Henry ever made. Henry made it just one year before he died.

Timeline

1898   Henry Moore was born in Castleford, Yorkshire on 30 July.

1906   The artist Paul Cézanne dies.

1910   Henry enters Castleford Grammar School on a **scholarship**.

1912   The passenger ship *Titanic* sinks.

1914–18 The **First World War** is fought.

1917   Henry joins the Army and fights in the First World War.

1921   Henry enters the Royal College of Art, London, on a scholarship.

1924   Henry's first **sculptures** are shown in London.

1926   The artists Claude Monet and Mary Cassatt die.

1928   Henry's first one-man **exhibition** in London.

1929   Henry marries Irina Radestsky and completes major work for London Underground.

1938   Henry takes part in the International Exhibition of **Abstract Art** in the Netherlands.

1939–45 The **Second World War** is fought.

1940   The artist Paul Klee dies.

1941   Henry is made an Official War Artist.

1940s   Henry has exhibitions in USA, Australia, Belgium and other countries.

1948   Henry wins International Prize for Sculpture in Venice.

1955   Henry is made a Companion of Honour in Great Britain.

1969   Neil Armstrong becomes the first person to walk on the Moon.

1977   Henry Moore Foundation begins work in Much Haddam, England.

1986   Henry dies in Perry Green, Hertfordshire on 31 August.

Glossary

abstract art   art that tries to show ideas rather than the way things look

bronze   type of metal

carve   cut into a shape

commission   being asked to make a piece of art

exhibition   public showing of art

First World War   the war in Europe that lasted from 1914 to 1918

graze   wander across a field eating grass

hollow   having an empty inside

miner   someone who works underground to dig for coal

roll of honour   list of names of people who have fought in a war

scholarship   money to pay for school

sculpture   piece of art that has been made out of stone, wood or other materials

Second World War   the war that was fought in Europe, Africa and Asia from 1939 to 1945

studio   special room or building where an artist works

tender   showing kindness and gentleness

More books to read

The history of Western sculpture: A young person's guide, Juliet Hestlewood, Belitha Press

More sculptures to see

Large Reclining Figure, Henry Moore, The Henry Moore Foundation

Two Piece Reclining Figure: Points, Henry Moore, The Henry Moore Foundation

Mask, Henry Moore, Tate Gallery, London

Index